T0124683

Out of the Darkness

The Michelle Bless Story

Michelle Bless

iUniverse, Inc.
Bloomington

Out of the Darkness

iUniverse books may be ordered through booksellers or by contacting:

iUniverse
1663 Liberty Drive
Bloomington, IN 47403
www.iuniverse.com
1-800-Authors (1-800-288-4677)

ISBN: 978-1-4620-8342-8 (sc)
ISBN: 978-1-4620-8344-2 (e)

Library of Congress Control Number: 2011963514

Printed in the United States of America

iUniverse rev. date: 1/10/2012

Out of the Darkness

Out of the Darkness

The names and places herein have been changed to conceal the true identity of the characters displayed. Be advised that the language and content of this book are very explicit and are intended for mature audiences only. This book is dedicated to my Lord and Savior Jesus Christ; it is he who directed me to write it as is—to tell the truth to set the captives free and give hope to the lost.

Chapter 1

Sold into Slavery and Meeting Satan's Team

Michelle has four other siblings (three brothers and one sister) and is the second oldest. She grew up in the northeastern United States. Several other siblings didn't survive the brutal beatings that her mother endured. In order to understand Michelle, you must have a peek into the family history.

I am Michelle. This is my story.

My mother was born in the Caribbean, and she had twenty-two siblings. Her father was a voodoo priest who molested all his children except her. My father rescued my mother after paying off my grandfather. The incest came out when my mother was visiting her parents. Concealed by a curtain, her brother was having sex with her sister, but when the curtain fell down, the incest was exposed. Brother and sister were having sex with each other, and the grandfather was molesting the boys and the girls. Mom was fifteen when she discovered this.

When my father had finished paying off my grandfather, my mom married him at age seventeen. Grandfather died when she was pregnant with me, and my mother was warned not to attend his funeral, but the family said that the baby she was carrying was sold to Satan as a curse. When she got to the funeral, they blew things in the air at her, but she paid no attention because she was busy looking at her father in the coffin.

A lot of her relatives on her father's side came to her and said she was carrying a girl (which was me), that I would have special gifts, and that I belonged to their God. My mom said she looked at them, thought no more about it, and walked away. She went to the funeral to be sure he was dead, but instead, without her knowledge, her attendance was just what they needed to enforce the curse on me because I was inside her.

My mom's dad and his sisters and brothers all worshipped the dark side and used various means to mark me for the dark underworld. Now, my father also came from the witchcraft world as well. My grandparents on my dad's side owned a farm, and the satanic rituals would take place there every summer. I spent time with my grandparents, and this is where my nightmare began.

My grandmother was unaware that my grandfather began to involve me in his satanic rituals and that he was molesting me. There were blood sacrifices and people wearing black hooded robes and lots of group sexual escapades. She recollects seeing a pentagram and candles. The priests would drink the blood of animals and of each other and the pigs, and they would rub the blood all over themselves and pour blood on each other when they would have sex. They would summon their demons by name, and they would levitate tables. There were all kinds of people who were pedophiles and rapists, but they didn't touch me because I was dedicated to Satan. My grandfather read the tarot cards and used the Ouija board. The men were molesting the women to impregnate them because my grandfather told them to do that.

From ages six to twelve, however, I was touched inappropriately by my grandfather and forced to satisfy his sexual needs and desires in every possible way. He threatened to use my sister if I didn't give him what he wanted, and so I never told anyone over the course of those sexual encounters. I had been taught by one of the women accomplished in the occult to have out-of-body experiences, and I would sit on the couch and watch my grandfather molest me.

Chapter 2

Battling Abuse from All Sides

The abuse I suffered from my grandfather seemed to be nothing compared to my father's physical abuse, which included things like the cold tub. I was to draw a full tub of ice-cold water. He would then submerge me in the water until I was completely wet; then he would pick me up by my feet and beat me with an extension cord till the tub was bloody.

He also beat my mother every day. We would try to stop him, but he would beat me and my other siblings whenever they tried to help. He would drag my mother up and down the stairs. We were never allowed to call him Dad; if we did, he would beat us. So we called him by his name because he never had a father to call Dad. He used broomsticks, ironing boards, and the barrel of a gun to beat us. Sometimes he would lock me in the closet.

My dad had an after-hours club in our basement, where I observed the people drinking. Many seemed able to laugh, giggle, and be happy. Some of the people would get up and try to shake it off; they would still be laughing as they fell and hurt themselves, but they continued to have fun. Apparently, what they were drinking made them feel better, so I wanted some.

I waited for the people to leave or pass out, and I would drink what was left in the discarded cups. I realized that the alcohol could numb me from the pain of the beatings, and I started to drink at the age of four. Nobody ever knew I was drinking, and I thought it was amazing. So whenever my father beat me, I would laugh at his beatings. He just thought I was crazy.

When I was six years old, the demons started to manifest to me. I knew they looked scary, but I was not afraid. The demons always had a vile, stinky smell, and I would tell them so. They were nice to me, and so they became my friends. The human spirits also came to me. I knew the human spirits were different because they didn't stink. They would just watch me and report back to Satan, as I later discovered.

I could see demons in other people's houses. I would ask them to stop my dad from hurting us, but they explained that they couldn't intervene. I could see demons walking with people sometimes, and the demons would urinate on them and put feces on them, and they wouldn't even know it was happening.

They told me to urge my mom to leave after one of her severe beatings. And then she would crawl on the floor through her blood and go to a small table in the corner of the room. There she would reach for her Bible and explain to me that she loved the Lord, and she would tell me to remember that Jesus loved me. I would say, "Who is Jesus? If he loves us, why does he allow my father to beat us the way he does?" I then developed a hatred for Jesus, and my mother realized that. She couldn't talk about Jesus around me anymore; she couldn't reach me.

One day I was sitting outside on our porch with the neighborhood kids. One of the kids asked why I called my father by his first name instead of Dad, and I said to them, "I can call him Dad whenever I want to." As I was saying that, my dad pulled into the driveway. And they dared me to say "Dad" when he got out the car. As he approached, the kids greeted him as Mr. David; my dad just grunted. I said, "Hey, Dad," and that's the last thing I remember.

I woke up from a fierce beating, lying on my back on the porch with a double-barrel shotgun to my face and my mouth full of blood. My nose was broken. My dad said to me, "Bitch, didn't I tell you not to ever call me Dad?"

I said, "Yes, sir."

He said, "Why did you call me Dad? And you better not lie."

I said, "The kids dared me."

He said, "If you ever call me Dad again, I will blow your motherfucking brains out—do you hear me?"

I said, "Yes, sir."

He said, "Get up and tell your mammy to take care of you. And throw that got damn dress away because I ruined it with blood all over it."

I went inside the house. My mother had seen everything. She took my dress off and held me and said she was so sorry. I told her it was not her fault and that one day it was going to be okay, and we would be all right.

I had always been very sheltered from other children, and I only had one friend, named Neese. One of the things that affected me the most was that I was teased by the other children because they made fun of my voice. They said I sounded like a boy but looked like a girl. My deep voice always felt like a curse, and I never understood why.

While in elementary school I was taught that black people came from apes, and white people came from the mountains, where they lived in caves; at least that was what my teacher told me. My father confirmed that theory to be true; he told me I looked like a monkey, and I believed it.

At age twelve I had a mature body and was completely developed. One day my dad sent me to pick up my sister from the half-day school, and a man dressed in army clothes (I later found out he was a bank robber) saw me and grabbed me. Luckily, I escaped his grasp. As I was running, a car struck me, and a neighbor looking out her window screamed, "Run, baby!" I survived and continued to run, still being chased by the man.

The neighbor called my dad and the police. I passed out, and my dad found me almost at the school. The only loving gesture I have as a childhood memory was him picking me up and carrying me in his arms with a blanket. He took me to my mother and then pursued the man—who was later found beaten nearly to death. The man was charged with bank robbery, attempted kidnapping, and attempted rape.

Chapter 3

Protecting the Weak

My aunt had ten kids, and my dad helped raise them because their dad was dead, and their mother was a stone-cold alcoholic. I sensed that my cousins started to be attracted to me, and they started to make comments to me that were inappropriate. I avoided them at all cost.

My grandfather started looking at my little sister, and I confronted him. One weekend while we were visiting my grandparents, he said to me, "Tell your sister to come upstairs."

For the first time I stood up to him and told him, "If you touch my sister, I will kill you dead—do you hear me? I will kill you dead." He just looked at me crazily with his eyes bulging out, and I went back downstairs and grabbed my sister and held her. My grandfather never mentioned that again, and I never left my sister alone when we visited. I always kept her with me, even when I went to the bathroom.

My grandfather met with his friends in the barn. I started to invite myself to the séances, and they all seemed to be afraid of me. I stopped coming to the rituals when I saw them preparing a sacrifice; I didn't see the actual sacrifice, but I knew it took place. When I confronted my grandfather about the children's whereabouts, he said, "I didn't see any kids, so shut up." I did remember seeing a child, but I just left it alone. I remember the kid was naked and in the same place where they performed all the animal sacrifices. My grandfather then told me that I was Satan's, and that was why I was never sacrificed. He used to say to me that I was special and very important, that Satan's followers were my friends, and that the demons were there to serve and protect me.

By the age of nine I had become the intercessor for my siblings and took the majority of the abuse so they would not be beaten as much. My father would come in drunk late at night, cussing and saying, "Bitch, where you at?" I knew he was talking about my mom, so I would be at the door waiting on him with my hands on my hips, and I would get smart with him. He started beating me for a while, and then he would fall on the floor and pass out. I would go in my room, and afterward my mother just looked at me and never said a word.

At the age of thirteen I became suicidal. When I talked to the counselors at school, my companion demon would direct me not to tell about the abuse and beatings because I would be taken away. The beatings for my brothers and sister and for my mother would go on and probably increase, and then my mother would probably be killed by my father if I did say anything.

Chapter 4

Demon Possessed

The hospitals would keep me when I actually started to attempt to kill myself. I would be visited by the demons and would be shown things while I was unconscious. I would be participating in sacrifices during my out-of-body experiences, especially during Halloween. In my spirit I saw people eating parts of people during my adventures in the underworld. My personal demon would escort me and tell me I should participate in the various rituals, which I refused.

I would be riding in the car with my grandfather and his friends, and I saw people sometimes hitchhiking or walking the streets. Sometimes my grandfather and his friends would abduct them; we would collect several people at one time. During this time he had stopped molesting me; I discovered later it was because I was being saved for Satan.

I discovered that I had powers that I hadn't known about. I would make statements in school about people who had made fun of me; for example, I would say, "Hope I never see you again," and they would disappear, or I would want their legs broken, and it would happen. It was my demon friends that made it happen, and my demons would tell me I had power. Although I had the ability to hurt people, I chose not to cause harm to the innocent.

The neighborhood boys started to notice me. One day at a neighborhood party, one of the boys tried to rape me, and my demons attacked him. They carried me home, only for me to later realize that my jaw was swollen. My daddy refused to take me to the hospital, so the next day my mother did. They learned that I had to have emergency surgery. I stayed in the hospital for eleven days because poison was found in my jaw, and it needed draining.

During my stay at the hospital, I would play games with the nurses and have the demons do things to them. My mother finally confronted me and said, "What are you doing to these nurses?" I explained it was my friends, and when I named them, my mother knew they were demons.

When I was thirteen, my grandfather was afraid of me and knew I had powers. While I was in the barn, my grandfather's friends and demons would say, "Commit to Satan," and then the demons would throw up and urinate on people, and they asked if I wanted to kill my daddy. I forbade them, because I wanted him for myself.

When I was fourteen, my dad called for me to come upstairs, and then he told me to tell my mother to fix him something to eat. I went to the bottom of the steps and said to my mom, "Your master said fix him something to eat."

He heard me and came running down the steps. He burst into the kitchen, where I was with my mom. He came up to me and said, "Bitch, what did you say to your mother?" and he hit me twice. I fell to the floor and then got back up and stared my dad down. He said, "Say what you said."

So I said, "Mom, your master said fix him something to eat." I said it loudly and nastily, and he hit me full in the face with his fist. I fell back the second time and landed in our big cupboard. This was where he had a tree trunk with a sharpened ax on it. I fell on the ax and started to bleed.

My mother screamed and grabbed me to check my back, but there were no cuts or anything. Then she let me go, looked down at me, and said, "Jesus."

My eyes turned black, and my body stood back up on its own. My dad looked at me, wide-eyed; then he said, "Ooh, forget this shit," and he walked out of the kitchen.

Chapter 5

Murder Witness and Seeking a Safe Haven

I turned to my mother and said, "I'm leaving."

My mother begged me not to leave, but I insisted that I had to go. Then she said, "He will beat me again," and I started crying. I said to my mom that if I didn't leave, I was going to kill him. The rage that was in me was strong, and for the first time in my life, I wanted to kill something; so I kissed my mother and left.

I walked the streets for hours. Finally I was picked up by a relative who was a street cleaner, and he took me to his sister's house. I stayed with this other cousin for a month during which time I fought off three uncles and my male cousin and barely escaped being raped several times.

During that time, one night while looking outside the window, I could see inside another house and observed a man beating and choking a woman. He had tied a sheet around her neck, and she was naked. The police were called, and they went in the house.

While I looked, they carried a body out and handcuffed the man. Then they went knocking on doors.

I told my cousin I had seen what happened, so when the police knocked on our door, she told them I had seen everything from the window. So they took me downtown and took my statement and told me that when the man went to court, I would be called to testify.

The man did go to trial, and I had to testify, but the man got off on the murder charge. His attorney twisted my story by asking me what color the sheet was that I saw tied around her neck. I said white. He laughed and said, "No, it was yellow." With that he got his client off.

Can you believe that? To me, that was crazy. I got so depressed as a result that I believed my grandfather when he said to me that nobody would ever believe me if I told on him and his friends. My uncles said the same thing, and so did my male cousins. That was why I shut down and never told a soul about all the things that were happening to me: I felt no one would believe me.

After that, the neighbor man constantly harassed me because I went back to my cousin's house right across the street from him. Then my cousin Tom called David, my father, and told him that they had me there and that they were afraid for my life because I had witnessed a murder. My dad came and got me, and he had a lot of dudes with him dressed all in black—caps, shirts, and pants. I later found out that they were his partners from up north. My dad belonged to a gang. They went and threatened the man, and believe me, that man did not bother me or my cousin's family anymore; in fact, within several days he sold his house and moved away.

At that point my father suggested I come home. He said to me, "By the way, your mama had a heart attack because of your black ass," which was how I found out. So I went to the hospital to see my mother. She was in ICU, and there were tubes attached to her and machinery everywhere. She begged me not to leave her again, saying the beatings had gotten much worse since I'd been gone.

I told the demons to slam the doors behind my dad in the hospital room. It scared him; and I told him that if he ever touched my mother again, I would kill him. My demons held him till he agreed not to touch her again.

Earlier, before I came home when I was out in the streets, I went to a teenage shelter where I met with a counselor. I told my story, how I had to hide in closets and all, but when they informed my parents that I was there, my father denied everything that had happened.

The counselors let me be a helper, and sometimes the girls would come in the office and talk to me. They always asked for me, and the counselors liked that because the girls would open up to me while they taped the sessions. That was because they really wanted to help, and I saw that.

One day, one of the girls, Tina, who had become attached to me, came to the office and wanted to talk to me, but this time I was busy on the crisis line handling a crisis call. She kept pleading to me that she needed to really talk, but she left the office, I would say, twenty minutes later. After I hung up, another girl came in the office screaming that Tina was lying on the bathroom floor bleeding. I ran to the bathroom, and, sure enough, there she was on the floor. The counselors pushed me away and tended to her. I knelt down beside her and kept saying to her how sorry I was that I didn't make time for her. Not only had the girl slit her wrists, but judging from the empty pill bottle lying next to her, she had also tried to overdose.

The ambulance got there and took her to the hospital. I made the counselor take me to the hospital. It was a close call, but she made it. They kept her in the hospital, and the counselor took me back to the shelter. All I kept saying was "It's my fault, it's my fault. I don't want to live."

The counselor directed me to go to my room and relax. "She did not die. Stop blaming yourself. It's not your fault. You were on the phone helping another kid, and one of us should have been in the office with you."

I went in the medical office, grabbed maybe thirty pills, went in the bathroom, and swallow them. The next thing I knew, I woke up in the hospital. They had pumped my stomach. The counselor demanded that I go back to the shelter with them. They were pissed. One of the counselors said to me, "We gave you a position here because you were so good with the kids, and now you did this. Well, go to your room; we will talk in the morning."

The next day I got up, sneaked out, and ran away back to my cousin's house. Now I was back home.

Chapter 6

Trapped at Home

My mother got out of the hospital a week later. When she came home, I stayed very close to her.

One day she and I were talking. She talked about her past. She told me about the time she and my dad had been married for only a year. My older brother was a baby, and my mother's mom and her sisters and brothers lived on one side of the house, and my mom and dad and baby brother lived on the other side.

There was a story about a house where the furniture and appliances were attacking the tenants, and the family was run out of the house. It was a big story; someone even died in the house. My mom, grandmother, uncles, and aunts moved in.

One day my dad and my uncle Carl went in the attic and found a bag of money that we later found out belonged to the spirits. That night when everyone was sleeping, my dad heard someone stomping up and down the steps. Next he heard stuff being thrown around in the attic. He ran up there with a shotgun with my uncles. Then, my mother said, they ran down the steps screaming. My dad grabbed my older brother and told everybody to get out of the house. They got outside.

My dad said, "There are ghosts in the house because things were thrown around by themselves with no one there, and *someone* was walking up and down the stairs, but no one was there." So my mom and grandmother laughed at my dad and uncles, and everybody went back inside.

But that wasn't the end of it. "Oh my god," my mother said, "dishes, pots, and pans were flying around by themselves, furniture moving around, lights flickering on and off." They ran outside again, and this time the police were called, and when they and the firefighters got there, they went inside the house and ran back outside, white as sheets, terrified. The police and firefighters were also being attacked. Finally the media got there. My mom said the news people filmed it, and the story is at the library in their archives. I just laughed because I knew what was going on. I knew they were demons.

One day I was outside with my friends, and one of them made fun of my voice. He said, "Your voice is so deep! You look like a girl but sound like a boy," and my friends all burst out laughing. He said it in front of a lot of people, and all the crowd came around roaring. I ran back home and shut down. I told my mom what happened and vowed I would never speak again. Even my friends no longer wanted to be around me because my voice was so deep and grew deeper. So for a whole six months I stop talking.

Then one day I was watching TV, and a tall white lady walked across the stage in a black-and-white gown. She said her name; it was Lauren Bacall, and when she spoke, she sounded like me.

I screamed for my mother. She came in the living room, saying, "What's wrong? Oh my god, you spoke."

I pointed at the TV. "Mom, that lady sounds like me."

My mother grabbed me and held me in her arms and said, "Thank you, Jesus. Thank you, God" (whoever he was).

In school I was the fastest runner, so my gym teacher said to me one day, "How would you like to go to the Olympics training camp?"

I said, "Yes, of course."

He said, "I will come to your home and talk to your parents." So that evening he did.

But when he knocked on the door, my dad said, all loud, "Who is this white man at our motherfucking door?" He told my mom, "Woman, go see who he is."

So she came in with my teacher, who introduced himself to David. He said, "Your daughter is one of our fastest runners in the school, and I can put her in training camp with the USA Olympic team this summer."

David said, "Hell no, she ain't going nowhere with you and no white people, motherfucker. Get the hell out my house." My teacher ran out and was gone. I had so much rage; I glared at my dad. He said, "You bring this white piece of shit in my house—go to your room." For the first time he didn't hit me.

My father refused to let me go to the Olympic team or run track because I was making money as a model, and I was made to count the money in our after-hours joint. That was my job, so I couldn't go anywhere but had to be at home. I felt stuck, trapped.

One day in elementary school, during the roll call, a girl asked me if my daddy's name was David. I said, "Yeah, why?"

The girl said, "Wow, Mr. David told me you were in my class. Your dad goes with my mom. He said you have a lot of money because he always says, 'I have six kids and a maid'"—referring to my mother as the maid.

I couldn't wait until school was over. I sat down in my seat with a rage burning inside me. At that very moment I wanted to kill my dad; I wanted him to die. After school I went home and told my mother what had happened in school. Although I knew about his many women, I had never shared it with my mom. It hurt my mother for me to find out like this and to know my dad called her a maid.

My mother started crying, telling me she was sorry. What was she sorry for? I said, "Mom, why are you saying sorry to me?"

She said, "I'm sorry you had to find out in school like that." And it was true, I was embarrassed in school, and I was pissed. I told my mom she had nothing to be sorry about. "It is not your fault. Dad is wrong; he is a dog."

Then my mom said, "Don't say that about your father."

I screamed, "He is not my father, and I wish he was dead!" Then I grabbed my mom and held her and said, "I'm sorry I screamed, Mommy. I'm so sorry." My mom just held me tighter. My father was a pimp, and he had many women. My hatred toward my father grew deeper.

Chapter 7

Working the Streets and Payback

When I was fifteen, another girl moved into another house behind my parents. Her name was Sheryl, and she was seventeen. She moved in with her grandmother because her mom had died.

My dad allowed me to hang out with Sheryl, her grandmother. Sheryl was very pretty. My dad used to tell me I was adopted—that I was found on a doorstep—because I was black and everyone else was light in my family. My mom used to tell him not to say that to me, but I believed my dad.

My friend Sheryl exposed me to a new world. She introduced me to some powerful men with money who liked to see me party. They used to take us out, and we snorted a lot of cocaine and popped lots of pills, and Sheryl smoked a lot of weed. Many new guys I met through Sheryl paid me to wear lingerie and dance for them. That's all I did, and it was to make some money because my dad took my paychecks from modeling and my part-time school job check.

From that point I started to introduce other girls from University College, and I started to turn them on to the game and make money off of their dates. Ultimately this made me a pimpstress. My dad had shown me how to run the game at sixteen, and I got paid on both ends.

I met a guy who didn't have a lot of money, but he was cute to me. I gave myself to him—and gave up my virginity—and got pregnant. When I told my mother, I thought my dad would beat me, but he didn't. Instead, he asked me if I wanted the baby and who the daddy was. I told my dad his name was Robert and he loved me. My dad told me to take him to Robert's house. I said he lived with his mom; he was eighteen, but he was in college and had a good job. I thought that would impress Dad, but it didn't.

He took me to their house, where Robert's mother offered for me to stay with them, but my dad refused. She was excited; after all, he was her only child, and she always wanted a grandchild. My dad said, "Hell no, I'm taking her home with me. She can have the baby at home." Then Dad grabbed me by the hair and took me home, and then he told me that he should have beat me to death. Then he left me standing in the living room with my mom, who stayed with me several hours.

Later my dad came back with a drink in his hands and said, "Bitch, you are getting an abortion, and I'm making you pay for it with your paycheck." I just looked at my dad because he was talking about my part-time job check, but he took my money anyway. He said he had already called the abortion place when we first got home—which was news to me and my mom. He told my mom to take me in the morning by ten o'clock.

I said, "I'm calling Robert."

He slapped me and said, "Don't touch my phone." He sat in the living room, watched me, and made me stay home. The next day he took us to the clinic. He told my mom she'd better not let me contact Robert to warn him.

I begged my mom, "Please let me call," but she was terrified of my dad and wouldn't let me.

At the abortion clinic, they took me in a room where I got undressed. They did not give me any medication but just strapped me down on a table. My mom held my hand. Then they put a tube in me and turned on a machine, and then this indescribable pain hit me so much that I passed out.

When I woke up, it was over. They gave my mom a prescription to fill. My dad came back to get us. We stopped at Walgreens; then at home, my mom gave me pain pills. I went to bed, and my dad said it was for the best. I told him I hated him.

My mom sneaked the phone to me, and I called Robert. He cried. My dad said my boyfriend couldn't visit anymore and thought our affair was over. However, I continued to see him in secret and, for the first time, experienced what I thought was love.

My girlfriend Sheryl wanted to skip school one day, and we went over to some guy's house. Sheryl left me at the house and went to the store. While she was gone, one of the guys that was at the house tried to rape me. I was able to get the guy to stop by telling him I had AIDS (of course I didn't), and then I ran downstairs and out of the house. I waited on the corner for Sheryl. When she came back and saw me outside, looking crazy, she jumped out of the car and asked me, "What's wrong with you, girl?"

I told her what had happened. She and her male friend went inside, and I heard them screaming at the guy who had tried to rape me. Of course he denied it; then we left.

Shortly thereafter my boyfriend Robert went into the navy, and I was heartbroken. We kept in touch. I started working down at the theatre part-time, but I became bitter and decided to become a pimpstress again. My primary clientele was very wealthy. I didn't believe in having oral sex, so I would let men give me oral sex only and let my girlfriends have sex with the men I set them up with. I wanted to have money and look like I was rich. My dad wanted me to still be a runner or do small errands, but I felt that it was a waste of time since I could make more money turning tricks.

In the midst of all this, there was a navy recruiter trying to get me to join the navy. He told me all he needed was one parent to sign the papers, and my mother agreed to, although she knew a severe beating would follow.

Chapter 8
New Location, Same Abuse

So I joined the navy, and for the first time I felt free. Two weeks after leaving for boot camp, I called my mom on the phone. She told me Dad had beaten her badly for signing me into the navy two weeks ago and that she was healing from her beating.

I was not good at taking orders and mouthed off at my superiors, which resulted in going to detention and made my workout extra hard. They couldn't figure out why they couldn't break me, but my martial arts background made it easy for me to withstand.

At the end of boot camp, I pulled a three-day pass. There was a white girl in my platoon whom I never got along with, and this made the white girl extra mad. Two other black girls and I bought officer uniforms that we were not legally allowed to wear yet. So we had a hotel room and then went to the officers' club. There we met some officers and started in on tornado drinks.

I must have gone into a walking blackout, because my girls later told me that at the club I'd started dancing and had taken off some of my clothes. I woke up the next day in our hotel room on my bed with money and phone numbers all over me in the bed, but I didn't remember a thing.

It was one wild weekend. I continued to party the next day, Saturday, and met another guy who wanted to marry me. Come Sunday he had clung to me like glue; then when it was time to go back to base, the white girl was there and tried to make us late. The white girl cornered me in the bathroom and tried to manhandle me into having sex, but I was strong and swift-flipped it around. I wrestled her to the toilet and put her face in the commode she had just taken a dump in, and the girl was defeated.

The next day the CO called me in and tried to charge me with assault, but another CO said, "No, let it go." They let me graduate that day. It came out that the girl had lied, and when it was thoroughly investigated, the charges were turned around. I graduated from boot camp and had thirty days to report to my new duty station.

When I flew home and got in the house, Dad was there, and for the first time, I could stand up to my dad. Because I was emancipated through the navy, I had no fear of him. I was able to give my mom money and take her shopping—and not tell Dad, because he also was a gambler. I visited all my old friends and clients so I could get paid.

I was the only black female stationed in my platoon in Louisiana. There were two other black women on the base, and they were both fine. I was a little jealous, and I teamed up with the light-skinned girl. We were chocolate and vanilla. The third girl was half Hawaiian, and she was pretty too. All the men wanted at least one of us. (I found out later that those girls were jealous of me.)

We were the three-way combination. The light-skinned girl I call a Jayne Kennedy look-alike. The Hawaiian girl was very naive, and the other girl and I had to train her.

I decided to date the marines instead of the navy guys. I made it known I was single, and I had all the men fighting for my attention. For the first time I was being treated like a queen, and I loved the feeling.

As time passed I noticed that my commander took a liking to me—like a father figure, or so I thought—and I didn't realize until later that he was out of order. One day I was alone at my desk, and my commander stood over me and asked me what I was looking for. I said, "Some change so I can get a soda pop."

He said, "Oh, I will get if for you. What kind do you want?" He came back and gave me the soda. It was open already, but I didn't think anything of it and drank it anyway. He suggested I leave and go back to my barracks, and so I did. He even came along and offered me a ride. I got in—and my next memory was of lying on my back with my commander riding me on top. I immediately went into combat mode and tried to kill him.

People in the barracks called the military police officers, "the MPs." The commander told them nothing was wrong, that I had gotten sick or something. He walked out with the MPs and left. I sat on the bed in shock. That was that.

I went to the hospital and had it documented. I saw the psychiatrist, and the doctor believed me. I even went and talked to a chaplain on the base, and he believed me too. But no action was taken; nothing happened.

I became depressed. I wanted to leave the military, but the commander wouldn't let me. I stopped combing my hair and began going to work with wrinkled clothes. People there noticed it. My commander came twice back to my room and raped me. He said I belonged to him and I was his nigger, and no one would believe me over him. He said I could make rank if I did what I was told.

One day at the barracks I was in the lounge, very sad. I met a navy guy who came over and befriended me. I told him I had no friends and missed home. He invited me to his family home because they were having a picnic. I didn't want to be in the barracks for fear the commander would return, so I went.

He introduced me to his family. They were very well off. I confided in his mother how my commander was continuing to grope me every chance he got at work and how he came in my room at night, raped me, and threatened me to keep me quiet, claiming that I belonged to him.

This woman listened to all my allegations and decided that the military was going to have to let me stay at her house with her other fifteen daughters. They drove to the base, packed my things, and took me back to her house, an eleven-room mansion. My commander was angry and knew I was gone the night before, because he had a key and was planning to rape me that night. He was so angry, he started to sabotage me from making rank so I would be stuck in a position where I had to continue to report to him. I fell back into deep depression, and I couldn't even groom myself.

The navy guy fell in love with me. He called me his girlfriend, and I felt like I owed him. After all, I felt as if he'd saved my life.

Then I became an MPO, a military police officer. I transferred temporarily with the military police force. I had a partner, and we were patrolling an officers' community. A white officer had just run over his wife with his car. When we got there, he was coming toward us with a knife. My partner said, "Halt!" three times; then I shot him in his legs to take him down. It felt good, but the other officers were mad because he outranked me.

But I didn't care. I had maintained contact with Robert, my boyfriend back home. I went to visit him in California. We spent a week together, and I didn't want to leave him, but I went to spend the second week of a two-week leave with my mother before returning home two months later. I paid Robert a surprise visit because he had given me a key. I walked in on him getting a blow job, and for some reason I didn't respond in anger. I just decided to pay every man back. Once I returned to base, the depression worsened.

The navy girls and I went out one night after partying with the two friends, and we were in a head-on collision. I woke up a month later, thinking it was the next day. I was released and sent straight to the main office, and they tricked me into signing myself out of the military. I then had to go through detox from morphine because I had been on it so long. I also had to learn to walk again, and the detox was very emotionally hard on me.

Michelle Bless

I later realized the paperwork I signed from the military stated I was a burden to the military and that I had hallucinated that I had been raped. I had to go to the VA every day and was referred to an attorney, who battled for me to get my proper settlement and discharge amended.

Chapter 9
Manipulating Men for Revenge

I reestablished my friendship with Sheryl and started kicking around men with means. I was determined to pay back all men for everything they had taken from me.

I met a guy in Ohio who was a drug dealer, and he taught me how to sell drugs. I was living with my parents, and they didn't know for a whole year that I had drugs in their house. My father never suspected that the large sums of money I shared with the family were gained from dealing drugs. I was still modeling part-time. There was still mental abuse taking place at the hands of my father, but the physical abuse had ceased because I was now a grown woman, and my brother wouldn't allow that to happen.

One day my father was in my room, went through my dresser, and found a briefcase I had hidden. When I came home, he was in the living room waiting on me with the briefcase open, looking all bug-eyed. He said, "I started to throw this out, but you're dealing with someone big, and I don't want to bring no problems back here, so get out with this dope and take it back to who it belongs to. Then you can come back." So I was forced to leave my father's house. I sold the dope as fast as possible and decided to get out of the game.

I later met a married man, James, who worked for the postal service, and I seduced him and became his mistress. He bought me a car, and I went back to my father's house. James was selling weed, and my uncle, who had introduced him to me, was selling powder cocaine. During this time I also sometimes lived with my friend Sheryl. I would get my boyfriend to get powder from my uncle, and I would help him sell his weed. I was partying and having a good time.

I also started seeing Robert, my cheating boyfriend from the military, who was now a civilian. I was now keeping him on an indefinite punishment. So all he got was played.

While clubbing I met my oldest daughter's dad, Tommy, and he swept me off my feet. I later realized I was with the first of my many obsessive and brutally abusive lovers. He was so attractive to me, and there were many women who wanted to date him. I had him; on the other hand, he was chasing me, and he was determined to get me. Slowly he worked his way into my life, and once we had sex, he was hooked. He was determined to have me carry his child. Although he had been with many women and could choose among many people to be with, I was his first true love. I was still dating several people.

One day Robert came by, tripping. I told him to leave and that I was not his woman. When I tried to break it off, he slapped me and ran out of my parents' house. I never accepted his apology, and we finally completely broke up.

Now Tommy, the fine-as- wine player, was still my main lover, but I was still seeing the married man also. One day I realized I was pregnant, and I was so sick. I had no idea who the father was. One night while lying in my bed in my lovely townhouse, furnished and paid for by my married lover, we were discussing the fact that I thought I was pregnant. He then revealed to me he had gotten a vasectomy, and the father could never be him. That's when I knew I was pregnant by my daughter's dad, Tommy. My married lover knew about him. He told me he would be out of town, so I decided to go over to my parents' house and visit for a while.

Tommy, in the meantime, had been calling me at my parents' house. While I was there, he kept calling, but I ignored his calls. He caught up with me finally by showing up. My dad let him in, so he begged me to talk to him. He was crying, and he picked me up, holding me tight. The motion made me queasy, although I usually liked it when he did that because it made me feel safe and reminded me of Tarzan and Jane. He was offended that I wanted him to set me down and asked if everything was all right.

I then blurted out, "I'm pregnant," and he was ecstatic and responded with such joy that I was completely surprised. I somehow had expected he would be angry, although he had expressed to me his desire in the past for a baby. He immediately called his mother and other family members to plan a dinner party to celebrate the good news and introduce me to the rest of his family. He told me how much he loved me, and I told him I was having an abortion. He was devastated and begged me on his knees not to abort his baby.

My mother walked in on the discussion. I was angry that she had found out. She asked Tommy to leave so she could talk to me. She reasoned with me and convinced me to keep the baby by reminding me of the abortion I was forced to have earlier. I resumed communication with Tommy a week later and informed him I would keep the baby but wanted to end the relationship with him because I didn't want to be in a committed relationship.

Meanwhile I was still seeing James and decided to tell him the same thing. He was furious. I explained to him that he was still married and that he couldn't control everything I did. He offered to leave his wife, and I didn't want that either. I liked being the other woman.

Eventually when the money ran out, I moved back home with my parents and told Tommy we could give it a real try. Tommy's family hated me, and they didn't believe the baby was his. His family envied the relationship we had and felt that I took him away from them. I found out dark secrets about his family, including the fact that several of his family members were shooting drugs—including him.

One day, while at his house, I was looking through a photo album and saw a lady that looked just like Tommy. When I asked him about her, he became very defensive and snatched the photo album. I continued to question him, and he finally admitted that the woman in the photo was actually him. He used to live as a drag queen and had done so for many years. He had lived and dressed as a woman and dated men for years. My response was devastation. I spit at him and ran upstairs. I called him several names. Over and over again, I screamed, "You nasty fag! I hate you!" In an attempt to calm me down, he grabbed me, and I lost my balance and fell down the stairs at four months pregnant. I had to be rushed to the hospital. The police questioned me, and I didn't have him arrested.

Upon my release, I went back home with my mother and continued to work at the post office and driving a truck until it was too much. When I delivered the baby, his whole family showed up and apologized for denying the baby. I moved back in with him, only to discover it was a big mistake. Another secret came out: the revelation that he had one of his main women from the past who had gone to prison for him.

She came to his house. I was in another room with the baby, but I could hear him talking to some woman; apparently before prison, she had lived with him. He responded to her with no concern for her return. I was pissed. I said, "First you were a fag, and now you got another woman." I threatened to leave, but he convinced me that their relationship was over, even though the woman had been sending him money from prison, which was beyond my comprehension.

I had already stopped having sex with him because I was scared that I would catch AIDS. I spent weeks living with that fear and continuing to be tested; I kept getting tested for the next fifteen years.

One day I came home from work, and two of his sisters were there with this woman. After his sisters nudged her, she said, "Oh, hi. How you doing?"

I went in the bedroom where Tommy was and asked him, "Who is that ugly, fat, black, bald-headed bitch sitting in my house who didn't want to speak to me? Doesn't she know I'm the woman of this house?"

He responded with "Well, I got to tell you something." I immediately knew it was the woman from prison. I calmly suggested he go out and talk to her, and then I proceeded to call my entire family, including my daddy. There was a knock at the door, and my whole family came to assist me in moving out. He called the police and tried to make me leave the baby with him. The police sided with me, and I left. After I moved home with my mom, I did allow Tommy to see his baby daughter, but the relationship was finally over.

I looked up my old girlfriend Sheryl and started partying again, and this time powder cocaine was a part of the festivities. I went back to my old married man, James, and he was so happy to get me back, he immediately started financing me again. I was selling powder and weed, and the money was starting to flow. After Tommy moved the woman out, he was allowed to pick up the baby. And between my mother and his, I had a lot of freedom to do my thing. I dabbled with pills like ecstasy and acid, but I didn't like it, so I continued to drink and do powder. Over time I had accumulated several sugar daddies, and one of them bought me a Mercedes. I was the ultimate player in my own eyes.

The party life was good and I stayed with it. As the years passed, I decided to take a break and went to a new city. While on the bus trip, at a layover I was hit in the back of the head and abducted. When I awoke, I was bound and tied to a bed. This man—I never saw him because I was blindfolded—kept me for three days. The first three days he beat me and had sex with me at his will. On the third day I convinced him to let me bathe, and told him I liked what he did. He insisted that he loved me and wanted to keep me forever. So he removed the blindfold, but after three days I couldn't focus to see right away. He assisted me in bathing, and I told him to go to the store and get me some lingerie so I could look sexy for him, and he did.

Everything was still a little blurry. I looked for my clothes but couldn't find them, so I grabbed the sheet and wrapped it around me. The door was locked, but there was a glass door leading to a patio, so I ran into the glass door. This only cracked it. Then I said the name of the god my mother always said to me growing up. I cried out, "God, help me!" and I put the sheet over my head and ran into the glass again, and this time it broke.

I was bloody but able to keep running and found myself on a back street. I flagged down a car. The driver was a black man who seemed to be caring and concerned about my situation. He gave me a ride as I explained what had happened to me. He then pulled over and said, "Since you've already been raped, I might as well get me some," and he proceeded to rape me. When he was done, he left me on the side of the road. I passed out when I saw the police coming toward me.

When I woke up again, I was in a hospital in the state of Ohio. My mom had put out a missing persons report on me. When I told the police what had happened and described the house, the police knew what I meant and took me there. They had apprehended the man who owned the house, and when they took me back to the house, they had him in a police car. When I positively identified the man, the police drove him away. I was taken to the hospital, and after a week they sent me back to Ohio.

I was reclusive and didn't talk to anyone. My mother called her church friends to pray over me, and they were shouting *Jesus!* which only made me mad. They anointed me with oil and rebuked the spirit of depression that had taken over my mind. My demon friend spoke to me; I hadn't heard from him in a long time. I laughed at those church women, and eventually they left my mom's home—and so did I.

I stayed here and there for weeks. One day I went downtown to visit my dad and noticed a man who wouldn't stop staring at me. I engaged in a conversation with my dad's friend, who was named Bobbie. My dad told me to pick out some clothes and jewelry. Recognizing the look that the man was giving me, I burned with hatred toward him and all men. I began to seduce him with my eyes and body, with every intention to do him in. Then Bobbie offered me a ride home; I didn't have one. By the next day, I had a Mercedes and was living in his condo. It was rare that anyone saw a black woman driving a Mercedes, let alone one that was paid for, and mind you, I was only twenty-three years old.

He insisted that he was in love with me and wanted my dad's permission to continue to see me as if I cared what my dad thought. He knew my dad was in the Black Panthers and didn't want to disrespect him. When we went to my dad, he said he already knew but granted permission because he appreciated him showing respect for Dad's authority.

Bobbie was older than me and had a legitimate day job, making $80,000 per year, and by night he was a drug lord. I had an inconsumable amount of cocaine at my disposal and all the money and clothes I could want and was still miserable. I had not had sex with him and after six months decided to give him some. In preparation I went to Planned Parenthood to get contraceptives and discovered, when they ran the routine test before dispensing birth control, that I was pregnant. When I received the news, I went hysterical, and they strapped me to the bed and called the police.

When I came to, they told me I had tried to stab myself. I told them I had been raped and sobbed uncontrollably. Once I told them everything that happened, the doctor said I was six months pregnant, too far gone for an abortion, but if I had five grand, I could go to Arkansas and get an abortion because such late-term procedures were legal there. I couldn't take that money out of Bobbie's stash and explain what I was using it for. I left and started walking home. Then I realized I was leaving my car, so I went back for it and drove home. I went inside and proceeded to drink and do cocaine to try to numb my pain.

I had not told anyone I was pregnant, so I tried to overdose on cocaine to kill the baby inside me. I would throw myself down the stairs over and over again. I even paid a drug addict to drop a TV on my stomach three times, and the baby continued to move. So every day I tried something to kill the baby.

One day a nun knocked at the door and introduced herself and asked if she could come in. She told me the clinic had referred me to her and asked again if she could come in. I continued to get high right in front of her. She started to minister to me about how the baby had not done anything to me. Eventually she comforted me and convinced me to stop getting high. She told me about the option to adopt. So she took me to her office at an adoption agency, and I picked out a woman to adopt my unborn baby. I wrote a letter that would accompany the baby when she was born.

I continued to have sex with my lover, Bobbie, who never knew I was pregnant.. I wasn't showing because I was carrying the baby in my hips and butt. I continued to have periods, and Bobbie never suspected anything.

Weeks later, after Bobbie got up for work, I started having pains. I waited till he left and then called my sister and the nun. My sister came and took me to the hospital because she lived up the street from me. She was shocked because no one in my family, including her, knew I was pregnant.

Immediately after I got in the labor room, the baby came, and I refused to look at her. There was an arrangement with the agency that I wouldn't have to see her. I had my mother call Bobbie, and she told him that I was sick, that she had found me passed out, and that he couldn't see me. Of course he agreed; he never questioned me.

The nurses changed shifts, and the new nurse didn't know I was not suppose to see the baby. I awoke, and the baby was looking at me, and all my hatred toward the baby melted away in that moment. It wasn't until recalling this very moment when writing this book that I realized: I finally allowed myself to grieve all the things I did to try to kill her. Realizing the hurt was gone, I couldn't part with the baby.

I notified the nun, who was very upset. I told the nun I had decided to keep my baby. The nun showed me the pictures of the baby's nursery and all the gifts the church had purchased and reminded me that this woman would be a better parent. My three-year-old had been visiting the baby, and I explained that she would be going away, referring to her baby sister. The nun took the baby, and I went home the next day and immediately had sex with Bobbie. I made a decision to destroy Bobbie simply because he was a man and part of the source of my pain. I started by cleaning out his bank account and taking a large portion of his cocaine stash. In one day I had cleaned him out. It was all in retaliation for slapping me two weeks before. I called my dad, and he came with a moving truck and some of his friends and moved me. I took my things to storage, gave my dad some money, and drove off.

I found out days later that Bobbie had put a contract out on my life; I told my dad, who told Bobbie that if anything happened to me, he would have him killed. That was enough to make him cancel the contract.

I hooked back up with Sheryl, and we were hanging tight. I stayed with her for a couple of weeks. One day I was walking around in our neighborhood and saw an old friend, Trent. He gave me a ride because I had let Sheryl drive my car to work. We started kicking it, and I convinced him to take me shopping. We became inseparable. I had the kind of sex that would make a man do whatever I wanted, and within two weeks I had a rock on my finger and was married. I got a job at AT&T, and Trent was working at a big company. We had it going on. I was not sexually satisfied with his loving, but he was a good man, and our relationship was okay. I decided to sell the cocaine I had left in Hamilton, Ohio, never return to dealing, and go straight. After a year he got hurt on the job climbing a telephone pole. He was on strong medications, and his doctor told me to watch him because in six months the medicine could give him severe mood swings and heavy blackouts.

One day, months later, he asked me where some money was that we used to keep in the house. I responded, "You know where it is." The next thing I remember was him calling my name, and then everything went blank.

I woke up, and I was broken up and badly beaten. My daughter was screaming (she was six or seven at the time). I felt very wet, and I wiped my face, but I was very woozy. I finally looked at my hands and saw the blood. I sat my daughter down, grabbed the iron lamp, and split him in the head with it. I ran out of the house with my daughter, and we jumped in the car and drove to the police station. The police came out from behind their desks when I came in the station with my daughter, and they were all in amazement when they took me to the bathroom.

I finally saw myself. My jaw was broken, my arm was broken, my nose was broken, and I was covered with blood. They rushed me to the hospital, and then a nurse called my friend Alice, so she could come and be with my daughter, because Sheryl was at work. In the emergency room I discovered I had fractured ribs and a head wound as well. I realized Trent had beaten me like that while I was unconscious.

The officer assigned to me, who was at the hospital, was angry and wanted to go pick up my husband. When they arrived, he had a candlelit dinner prepared for me. He was in complete denial; because of the medication, he didn't remember a thing. He was arrested on a Friday, and I was released from the hospital.

Alice took me home; Tommy came and got our daughter for me to take care of her for a while. Alice and I proceeded to get high until a knock came at the door. It was my husband's aunt and his mother. His mother saw the devastation of my beating. My mouth was wired shut, my arm was in a cast, and I was covered with bruises. His mother suggested we get a divorce and asked if she could retrieve some of his things. I refused to let his aunt in because she was aware that I knew she harbored a lust for her own nephew, my husband. We visited her and she knew we were coming; she would be dressed in a see-through nightgown, with no under garments on. I never was receptive to her, and I had a gut feeling she wanted to take him to bed. Once his mother gathered some clothes for Trent, I insisted she leave since she had his nasty aunt waiting outside, and the fact that she had even come along was repulsive to me.

Alice left, and I called another friend. I consumed large amounts of alcohol, even with my mouth wired shut, and was drunk. While driving drunk I noticed out of my rear view mirror there were fifteen police cars pursuing me. A policeman had to help me out of the car after he saw all my injuries. They took me to the police station, and everyone felt so sorry for me, they dropped the charges.

By Monday I was in front of a judge and filing for divorce. My husband was brought in, and he didn't want a divorce. He pleaded that it wasn't his fault because of his illness. I said it didn't matter; he had beaten me in front of my child, who recounted everything he did while I was unconscious. I reminded the court that his next blackout could mean my life. I wasn't willing to take that chance. The judge granted the divorce.

I went into a heavy party mode after I healed from my injuries. One day my friend Alice's brother Derrick noticed me, and since

Alice was too drunk to go out, I went out with her brother. We went to several clubs in Kentucky, and the night progressed; we were doing powder all night and drinking. We went back to my house, and that's when he introduced me to crack.

I liked how it made me feel. He didn't tell me it was crack. We had incredible sex, although I had to teach him what I liked. By the end of the night he was asking for mercy. We continued to get high, and I wanted to get more of the dope the next day. My girlfriend Alice got jealous because her brother and I began to spend more and more time together. My ex-husband continued to beg me to forgive him and come back, but I refused and turned deeper to my drugs and party life.

One day I pressured Derrick to go get me some more drugs. He didn't want to go, so I went to a well-known drug area to make a buy but got fleeced. I left and quickly returned to the drug dealer and hit him with a baseball bat. I took all his dope and money. I did it completely out of anger.

For some time I continued to get high and function on my job. I had a friend who used to be involved with Derrick, and she was jealous of our relationship. Alice and Derrick 's mother both loved me. Alice's family found out that Derrick had turned me out on crack.

A few years passed before the unmanageability of the addiction started to take a toll, and I finally lost my home and eventually my job. While on unemployment I continued to get high. I was living with Derrick's mother, but she wanted me out. She made arrangements to get me another apartment because she didn't have the heart to just put me and my daughter out on the street.

My new landlord had been a man before having a sex change. She was a mean slumlord, but she gave me an apartment. We would have verbal altercations, and I would tell her about herself and remind her that she wasn't really a woman. While living there I didn't allow Derrick to move in. He had become a complete leech.

All my old connections now knew I was getting high and wouldn't deal with me anymore; I couldn't even get modeling jobs. I started going to get other people their dope to help supply my habit, and I had dope dealers who gave me fat packs with enough for me to get high and still give my clients a nice amount; that way they wouldn't question whether I had taken anything. My whole life was revolving around getting high. I had my daughter only every once in a while, but she was spending the majority of her time with her dad.

I slowly gained a little weight back and was able to get a modeling job. I was able to model off and on because they liked models extra skinny, and I could fix up my face with makeup. One day, when coming from a modeling job, I met a man named Jim. Jim saw me at a distance walking and made a U-turn to catch up with me. He claimed love at first sight.

He was like a knight in shining armor. He showered me with love and attention—or at least what seemed like love. For years we kicked it together, and when I would go off on my drug binges, he would drive around for hours looking for me. He rescued me from dangerous situations from time to time, and he didn't know I was hooked on crack, because I was a model and had mastered covering up my addiction.

One day he moved me out of my apartment into his house because he wanted to keep a closer watch on me, and that was the beginning of a nightmare. He became very possessive and didn't want me to work. Instead of being compliant, I got two jobs. He took me to work and picked me up. He smothered me, and I had to take days off from work just to get high. My addiction to Jim was in its highest peak. I eventually had to quit one job and then lost the other job because of too many absences. I was given a choice to resign or be fired, so I resigned.

After I found another job, I started to leave the house. When I went to work was when I got high. I still continued to model part-time, and I saved enough money to get my own apartment. I found a place to stay, and as I started to scout out the new neighborhood, I met a minister who lived in the area. I figured out the preacher was smoking crack, and he started using my house as a spot to get high.

One night I left the preacher with my daughter for five minutes, and during that brief time he raped her. She didn't tell me immediately, but the next day she passed out at the bus stop, and she wound up at the hospital. The whole thing landed in court. It turned out he had been molesting his stepdaughter, and there emerged pictures and video of him having sex with her from ages two to thirteen. He got forty years in prison. I told the judge that if they let him out, he would be killed. Although he went to prison, I had a family member in jail rape him while he was there. My daughter stayed in the hospital for a week; after she came home, she was homeschooled for the rest of the year. The next year I asked her father to keep her for a while, because I realized I was unstable.

I went deeper in my drug addiction and was evicted several times and labeled a nuisance. I slept on park benches and in abandoned buildings for a long time and ate out of garbage Dumpsters. I would go behind restaurants and eat the leftovers from the garbage; meantime, I was nursing my nerves with more and more drugs. I was no longer working and received income from my ex-husband and unemployment. I was also doing stickup jobs; I would also rob tricks using vaccine and put drops in men's drinks and put them to sleep. When I did have steady money coming in, I would smoke it all up and have to go back to eating out of nearby Dumpsters in between checks.

I sued my landlord and got $5,000 for damages from a leak. I fabricated all these clothes that were supposed to be ruined by the water damage. Eventually he evicted me, and I moved back in with Jim. During that time I would go to abandoned buildings to get away from him so I could get high in peace. It cost me a thousand dollars per day to get high. I moved out again and found another place that was twenty-five dollars a month. I sold everything I had; this was the beginning of my very bottom. One day I got butt naked in an abandoned building for a trick, and it was very degrading to me.

One day I went to see my grandmother, and I got mad at her because she wouldn't let me eat something at her house. I left, and my grandmother called me for three days but I wouldn't return her call. Then she died—and I had a nervous breakdown. I started renting rooms to the dope men, and they took over my place. The next month I got evicted, and I became completely homeless.

I called my uncle, who wouldn't take my clothes to his house, so I just grabbed a bag and walked the street. I was forced to call Jim, and I moved back in. Things were very different. Because he knew I was a dope addict, and because he was hurt, he hurt me back in the worst ways. He would lock the refrigerator and cabinets and wouldn't feed me. I finally left and went to a shelter, the drop-in center, and the first night I was raped. I ran outside in the rain and fell and broke my ankle and wound up at the hospital.

I then called Jim to go back home. This time he left me in the hallway entering our house and departed for work. I became suicidal and tried to kill myself. There were dark purple curtains in the hall; no light could come through them, but yet a big, bright light beamed through. I couldn't figure out how that was possible.

Then came a voice that didn't sound like my friend's voice I used to hear when I was a child. It was different, very calm. The voice said to me, "Go to that lady who was good to you, who is up the street. Remember the time she fed you and gave you Kroger gift cards, that day when you were hungry?"

So I grabbed my crutches and headed up the street. I passed a little church, but I heard a voice in my head telling me not to go to see the female minister. The voice told me she would laugh at me—make fun of me after all I had done—and that I smelled bad from being raped the night before, when I was locked out of my house by Jim.

So I turned around to walk back to the house, and the voice was telling me to take the pills to end my life and stab myself. As I was walking I noticed a lady coming from the steps of a church, and she saw me and called out, "Excuse me, come over here so I can pray for your leg," because I was walking with crutches. I had two black eyes that were shielded by sunglasses. I said to her that prayer would not help me; the next thing I knew, she ran across the street. I tried running, but my broken ankle wouldn't allow me to.

She eventually caught up to me and grabbed me and said, "Prayer will help you." After she touched my shoulders, I fell into her arms and felt peaceful and safe, a feeling I'd never felt before. She welcomed me to her church; I hesitated but couldn't resist what I was feeling, so I followed her.

As I walked, I heard the voice telling me not to go. "I'm your friend; don't go with her." The voice changed from an eight-year-old to a deep male voice and screamed at me: "Didn't I tell you not to go in here?"

The lady got me to the top of the steps, to the threshold of the door, and took me in.

TO BE CONTINUED in Book 2: Battling the Darkness.

Feel free to contact me at:
outofthedarknessministries@yahoo.com